the fall, the rise

MAIA

www.maiapoetry.com

Cover & Illustrations by Pride Nyasha Mapfumo

ISBN: 978-1986827560

i hope you find your way here
i hope you get lost
but
i hope you find your way

the fall

they ask
why do you still miss him?

i say
i was drowning
but eventually
everyone misses
the ocean

i love you as if you were here
as if you weren't the wind
or summer leaves
but as if you were cement
and that is part of the problem
loving something
that has already left

i have been told
do not let the world
make you hard
time
and time
and time again
but i am stacking bricks
pouring concrete
shaping locks
building fortresses
against the very same people
who spoke those words
and who have made
the world
hard

there is so much of me
overflowing into you
i cannot tell
if these are my lips or yours
if these are my hands or yours
i cannot tell

i am drowning in you

the silence at two in the morning
is what breaks me the most
i remember when your laughter
filled my room and tugged at my skin
reminding me of how much
i was in love with you

i step in the shower
and i rinse you off
i watch you fall down my arms
i watch you fall down the curves of my hips
i watch you fall down my legs
if only it was that easy
to stop loving you
as easy as it is to rinse you off
after loving you

i am aware that when the sunset falls
the sky turns black
and there are many stars
to gaze in awe at
but i was hoping
that maybe
just maybe
you'd see mine

i am a star
can you see me?
i am only trying to light up the sky
for you

i lean into you
and i fall
like a child off of the swing
like a book off of the shelf
like a glass off of the table
accidentally
suddenly
and all at once

the fall

i have heard many times before
that you should be
careful
that you should
wait
that you should
look both ways before crossing the street
but all i ever saw
were green lights in your eyes
and crosswalks to your heart
and i forget all the silly rules
and the miles per hour signs
and i drive
full speed
into you

i do not dwell in a world that is black and white
i was not born colorblind
but i was living in the dark
then i saw you
and you became
my
favorite
color

you asked me
do i miss you
i step on the witness stand
you patiently wait for the verdict
the jury is hung
and i plead the fifth

did
fear
lead you back to me?

or
love?

i want to know

i have a thing for the forgotten
forgotten books
forgotten places
forgotten people
i have hands full of love for them
i took you in and i showed you
that i remembered
and now you've gone
i, too, have become a forgotten thing
and i don't remember how to remember me
i have no love left
for myself

all i'm asking you to do
is notice me
i'm right here
i have always been
right here

please tell me you did not forget
about my smile
because all i can remember
is that yours lit up the room
and it has been endless nightfall in mine ever since
please tell me that you did not forget
about my eyes
because all i can remember
is how i used to feel at peace when i looked into yours
and i've been restless ever since
please tell me that you did not forget
about my hands
because all i can remember
is that yours gave me a reason to hold on
and i've been drowning ever since

the moon settles in
and so do i
incandescent light
hugs my skin
it lets me know
tomorrow will be here soon
and to hold on
for just a little while
longer

i am sorry
(but not so much sorry)
if this is an ultimatum
between loving you
or loving me
you should not have to ask
i will always choose
me

because by choosing me
i will always
choose you

you were everything
i wanted you to be
and that was the problem

everything

you would always say things far too late
and i always held on a little too tight

maybe it was how the rain hit the pavement
the night you told me that you loved me

maybe it reminded me that things can still be *good*
even when it is pouring

but you didn't really love me, did you?

i love the smell of fresh flowers, but even they
wither away

and the pavement, it dried

and everything that seemed like it was

wasn't

the ocean sighs
as it ebbs and flows
as the waves crash
as the sun sinks down
and disappears in it
it'll be back
and i sigh too, with it
he won't

you made a home out of me
you lived here some
and you lived elsewhere others
when you were here
i made you feel safe
comfortable
i sheltered you
embraced you
kept you warm
but why didn't you tell me you were only renting?
i forgot myself
you were never good at long-term contracts
anyway

tenant

he destroyed me
i said
how
they ask

by having hands that loved me
but a heart that didn't

love was not that great of a friend to me
it bought a one-way ticket
boarded the train with time
and has not returned
since

please
just let me go
you look at me as if anything
is better than nothing
but how many times do i have to tell you
that i want to be *something?*

before i knew it
your lips met mine
all of a sudden
home
had a new meaning

i walked through my front door
and i saw loneliness
sitting there
waiting for me
to embrace her on the couch
and every day
when i walk through my front door
she is there
waiting for me
sitting in the same dented
worn-in spot
you used to sit in
and some days
some days
i embrace her
i lay my head down on her lap
and i think of you
i look to my front door
i know love will be here soon
but for now
she
is all
i have

i held onto him
for the first time in a long time
after you
i clung to him like lip gloss stains on collars
in parked cars under street lights
i felt on him like the wind brushed up against
the leaves, how it is supposed to
because i was supposed to
i tried because i had done it for so long
before you
but my hands did not hold him
quite like they held you
my bed did not feel
quite as warm as it should have
we did not make magic out of our love
quite as good as we should have
and in the morning
the sun did not come peek in the room
quite as bright as it used to
but i held onto him for dear life
and honestly, truthfully
i was praying and hoping
somewhere inside of him
inside of those arms
inside of those lips
inside of those temples
i would find
you

he is not you

i have cried oceans to sleep
wondering what i ever did
to deserve such heartache

i knew heartbreak was not
a pretty thing
but i did not expect it to unravel
all of my insides
shatter my heart
crack open my spine
in search of you
to drain you out of me

the release

my bed reminds me of you
so i sleep on the couch
all of my sheets remind me of you
and i wrapped up into them
love leaking all over them
so i sleep without them
and i will be here
sleeping without them
as long as i am sleeping
without you

these nights
i do not get much sleep
in my dreams
i always see you
and there is nothing wrong with that
you have always been my favorite thing to look at
but i do not want to see you
just in my dreams

i am beginning to miss the days
where i did not have to dream
to see you

we were like broken clocks
stuck in time
looking for others
to repair us
and neither one of us
wanted to be the first to run out
even though we knew
what we had
was already
long gone

i loved you once
he uttered
do you think i could love you again?

i sighed
if this was right
you would still love me
now

the fall, the rise

i first met you in a coffee shop
the world slowed
our shoulders brushed
the lights flickered
and you smiled
home, i thought

we ended on the corner of 3rd and 4th
the world slowed
our hands unclasped
the sky flickered
and you held your head and asked
where do you want to go now?
home, i thought

sometimes
i cannot handle it all
i stuff it down, down
in a box
and i put it on the shelf
not tonight
not tonight

i heard knocking
at my front door
it sounded a lot like
the pounding in my chest
since you left
i opened the wooden door
i've used to keep myself from the world
and it from me
and there you stood
i suppose all the roads
you thought you wanted to follow
emptied you out onto my front porch
you looked bruised
and a little broken
i wouldn't dare say
i told you so
i let you in
and i bandaged you up
just as
i always did

i heard the day closing
a cracking in the sky
dusk laughing
as the night began to fall
moon
have pity on me
you know how i get
on nights like these

i have been fighting battles
all this time
with the world
pushing them out
keeping myself
in
at bay
preserved
and intact
and when i get home
i stand in front of the mirror
i see cuts on my cheek
bruises on my temples
oh
i have been fighting myself
all along

end of summer
fireworks rang in my ear
they crackled and popped
it sounded a lot like my heart breaking
i closed my eyes
and i let the sound waves pulse into me
and through me
the crackling
the breaking
all of the sudden
it felt good
it was magical
to break
for once

night 1
this isn't so bad
the silence is deafening
i could get used to
the white noise

night 5
i'm starting to miss you
and the way your lips felt pressed against mine
at twelve in the morning
times where we had no business being awake
but we were anyway
just to catch one last glimpse of
each other

night 10
i am broken
and you took all the pieces with you
i did not know loneliness could feel like winter
in my room
the snow is falling
it's piling up on my nightstands
on my dresser
barricading me from the world
i wonder if you knew
loneliness would eat me alive
and consume all the parts you
liked most about me

i wonder if i'm somewhere
anywhere
intertwined in your thoughts
because at least if i am anywhere
i am there

night 20
i stand under my door frame
gazing at my ruffled sheets
and thinking how i do not want to
embrace myself in them
if you're not under them waiting for me

night 30
well you have not called
there is no longer silence
i turned my thoughts up loud
and the music even louder
the snow melted
i washed the sheets
i no longer wonder
if you're thinking about me
i just wonder
about you

i had a man
who left me as quickly as he came to me
almost like how
the sun leaves as quickly as it rises
beautiful
yet taunting

greed dripped from your lips
and i mistook it all for love
and now you have gone
to another to satiate your thirst
but i am still here
arms stretched and palms cupped
hoping i catch whatever
is left

you
were the only thing
i fell into
without the fear
of the fall

you asked me how i felt about all of this
you asked me to spill my heart out to you
to lay it all on the table
as if my heart was water and i the glass
i laughed and tilted my head
you are a gift after a long path of heartache
the enchantment standing there
waiting for me at the end of it all
you are light, the brightest of them
that i've seen yet
you are flames
that i wouldn't think twice about rushing into
you are rivers wide and oceans deep
full of mystery and the things
you don't want your closest of hearts
to know about
and still
i wouldn't mind
bathing in your hurt
your past, your pain
i wouldn't mind pulling you out of the depths
even if it meant sacrificing myself
i wouldn't mind loving you
until water runs dry
and the mountains fold
and the world collapses
and yet
you asked me how i felt about all of this
you asked me to spill my heart out to you
i laughed and tilted my head and said
i don't feel anything

at all

the room is still
the house creaks
the world silent
i look at you
next to me
i feel your love
leaving me
it is pacing
at the front door
pondering
if it should stay or go
i won't beg
for it to stay or go
but just know
i will love you
either way
all the same

i do not know how to love someone
with a glass half full
i only know of love as
pouring into their cup until it runs over
because i was too busy
falling into the creases of their mouth
falling into the depths of their eyes
falling into the warmth of their arms
falling into love

i can't do it anymore
i say

do what
he asks

look at you and try to pretend
i don't see the whole world

honesty

i am in love with a man
that is not mine to keep
he leaves an imprint in my bed
he leaves his soul wrapped up
in my sheets
his scent lingers
on my pillows
on me
i am half full when he is near
and half empty when he leaves
his laughter echoes in my mind
his smile sits in my eyes
his being bears down on my chest
and reminds me
he is not mine to keep
but i am still in love
with a man

you pulled feelings out of me
and then scolded me
for letting them fall on you

my mind knows
this will come to an end soon
a screeching halt
my heart knows
that i am still full
and still content
with the time spent
i can wholeheartedly say
with sadness welling in my eyes
that i was grateful
to know you
but even then

i will miss you, i will miss you

i felt the break coming
and even though
you can brace for impact
that does not mean
you will not feel the crash
and it does not mean
you won't shatter
anyway

how am i mourning
the loss of you
when you still walk
the same earth as i do?

you should be with me

before you
i believed wrong was wrong
after you
wrong has manifested
into so many rights
and now i believe
that sometimes
wrong has a way
of telling us
something
is
right

wrong vs. right

you are running out of
i'm sorry's and we are
running out of time

i still look for you
in crowds
in the places we used to go
in the skies
the stars
and the moon
i still look for you
and wherever you are
i hope you are looking
for me too

are you?

MAIA

there are things in this universe
i will never understand
like how it sent you to me
without you being *ready*

everyone
who i think may be *the one*
ends up leading me
back to you

what if i told you i was a flood?
i cover everything in sight and
leave destruction in my wake
would you be okay with that?
would you drown in me?

you are everything my hands have
been longing to hold
i promise
i won't drop you
i don't want to let go
just yet

you were good
at everything
you did to me until
it came time
to love me

i can still feel you on me
what i wouldn't give
to rid myself of this skin
so that i can rid myself
of you

shedding

wherever you are
i hope the world is
kind to you
and i hope you *love*
even if you didn't
trust your heart enough
to love me

you ask me what i want
but you have to know
that it has always
been *you*

it will always be you

it was something about the way you said
you need to stop giving so much

i don't know how
you see the world in black and white
and i would rip my eyes out if i could
to let you see the hues
our bodies paint when we are mixed together
i would give you my hands
to let you dip your fingertips into the shoreline
so you could see that even the softest things
can still remain after being crashed into
for so many years
i would give you my legs
to let you sprint up to the mountaintop
and witness the grand finale of every day
and that the sun, too
gives and asks for nothing in return

i don't know how
to stop yearning for you to see our colors
i don't know how
to stop being as soft as sand
i don't know how
to stop the light from pouring out
even when others have tried to seal the cracks
i don't know how

we are
consistent
with the things we want

i suppose
that is why i waited
by my door every night
and why
you never came

the clocks in my house all read 3 A.M.
but they must all be wrong
usually at this time
i would roll over and see you
usually at this time
you would wrap your arms around me
usually at this time
you would hold me so tight
that i could barely even breathe

now at this time
i can barely catch my breath
now at this time
i am clutching the pillow you slept on
now at this time
i am reaching for something that left
now at this time
i roll over and brace for the breaking

here i am
putting my heart onto paper
treating ink as if it were love
hoping somewhere
wherever you are
you can feel it
through the pages

can you feel this?

my legs are shaken from falling
and never being caught
and i am convinced my eyes are failing
because you were not
who i thought you were
tell me i am not going colorblind

love used to be my favorite color

it is hard
but i live anyway
some nights
i am all tossing and turning
tear-stained pillows
praying for a way out
running from loneliness
but ending up in the hands of fear
i am afraid that you can't help me
i am afraid that maybe you can
every time i believe i have learned
to put one foot in front of the other
i lose my balance and fall into the depths
the oceans of the nights i spent weeping
and i am swimming away from myself
but ending up in the jaws of you
it is hard
but i love anyway

i laid down next to a man
because his silhouette looked a lot like yours
and i couldn't tell if it was you or him
in the dark so i figured
he would do

but my breathing grew weaker as i held my breath
because he didn't smell like you
and i flinched because his hands
didn't hold me like yours did
who am i fooling?
we both know
anything other than loving you
is nothing short of a disappointment

the notches in my bedpost
are from the men who left me scarred
the men who used my body
for temporary worship
to numb their own pain
in search of peace
and the cries at two in the morning
are from me remembering
that i let them

sometimes
i forget about you
but only for a second

i lie in my bed at night
dreaming of your silk-woven
skin pressed against mine
your half-smile that shined
a little too bright and left
the moon and i squinting

i lie in my bed at night
and it's cold
there is no warmth here
not the kind of cold that could be
fixed with fires and wool-spun jackets
the kind of cold that leaves you
and your heart shattered
on the floor next to your nightstands

sometimes i forget about you
but only for a second
and after a second
i am counting all the
seconds, minutes, and hours
wondering if i
and this shattered heart of mine
will ever be warm
again

the sun and i are one in the same
the sun burns
for its world
and i burn
for mine

you

it's not completely your fault
i wasn't looking where i was going when i fell into love
i let it submerge me
i let it drown me
and when i came back to life
you were the first thing i screamed for
as if you weren't the reason i drowned in the first place

see, love is twisted
it invites you in with its open arms and warm skin
freckled with the possibilities
of not leaving you completely and utterly broken
and then, it stomps out your fire, rips open your heart
and bleeds you dry of anything it ever gave you
but you see, love is not always as twisted
that was love when i loved you
loving you was waiting for the sunrise
and getting rain in return
it was open hands in mercy
and receiving scars for ever doing so
it was being drowned by the person who once
gave you a reason to hold on

but love told me you weren't it

and now
with bruised hands and trembling legs
i believe her

it sounds silly
but i look for you everywhere i go now

as if you're something comparable to stars
and i just might see you everywhere
only if i look up

but i look for you everywhere
hoping maybe their lips will manifest into yours
or the words they say
will sound as good as they did when you said it

but right now
it's 3 A.M.
and i'm looking over at the man
lying next to me
and i'm looking up
and i can't find you
anywhere

i am sharpening my sword
on your stone-cut teeth
you are all razor blades
and i am no match
for the games you wish to play
tongues are made for soothing
but yours drips hatred
on the floor
leaving puddles
of the love i thought we had
around my feet

the battle you've already won

some nights
i drive as far away
as i can
all of these city lights
remind me of you

joy rides

i tell him
i was whole once
but my pieces are stuck
in other men
ones i gave away
because they did not fit in my hands
the way i wanted them to
ones i gave away
when i hated the body i was living in
but he looked upon me
as if i put the sun in the sky
ones i gave away
because the one before
said that it was his least favorite
ones i gave away
just to see
if they would give any
pieces of themselves
back

we gazed at sunsets
that didn't want to give up the sky
i looked over at you
and realized i was the sun
and you were the sky

i don't want you to go
but i don't want that
to be the only reason
you *stay*

i need to hear it
i need to hear you say
i don't love you
tell me
so what's left of my heart
can finish breaking

so i can start rebuilding myself, again

the trees are bare
and so am i
i suppose this is how it feels
losing something
that used to love you

curling up
in someone else's arms
is foreign territory
and i just want to go
home

in another life
we are patiently waiting
to realize that we are made
for each other
in this one

even when
i had nothing left
you still took from me

what kind of love is that?

you are a sea
i would not mind drowning in

how do i move on
when i thought you were
my last stop?

i don't mind
writing poetry about you

these words are the closest
i'll ever get to you
again

one day
i will stop peeling back
the layers of your flesh
over your heart
searching for a forever
to get lost in

i know
that you feel this too
tell me
i am not alone here

nights like these are when i wish
i could turn back time, not to change anything
perhaps not even to meet you sooner
that's like saying i want to change fate
and i don't

but nights like these are when i wish
i could go back to my summer body
when you were all over me
and the air wasn't the only thing that was hot

nights like these are when i so desperately
want to be lying in your arms
perhaps talking your ear off about dreams
and the universe or not talking at all
and just reveling in the fact that i get to breathe
the same air that you do

nights like these are when i wonder
if you know that i feel like
these lips are made for you
that my hands are just the right fit for yours
that the cavity in my chest might be where you are
supposed to live

i wonder if you know that i think it could be *you*
this is me falling out of perspective
and jumping into the oceans of my heart
but baby these are fair seas

sometimes i wonder if you know
sometimes i get so upset that it rains in my room
sometimes i get angry at myself for falling
without anywhere to land
sometimes i don't care because i'm grateful
to know you
sometimes i wonder
how lucky i would be
if it was *me*
that got to love you

please let it be me

i am no stranger
to loneliness
but i should not feel alone
when i am next to you

love should not feel like this

i tripped over a rock the other day
that takes me back to the time
when i fell
and you weren't there to catch me
i stumbled once and you didn't blink an eye
i didn't trust you after that

that takes me back to the time
when i gave you my all and then a little more
and you didn't blink an eye
i wasn't whole after that

that takes me back to the time
when i thought it was all over
and when i couldn't take the pain
when sorrow hung around my neck
and strangled me until i became new again

see
even when it has nothing to do with you
it has *everything*
to do with you

the fall, the rise

i wonder if you know
i would cross the sea for you

i tried to get you to stay
the love in my lungs was not enough
even though you knew
you were my favorite air to breathe

i dug myself into this earth
i know how much you love dirty things
maybe if you saw me as the beauty
that comes from that same soil
you would stay

i even pulled the sun out of orbit
to show you that it could be yours

but you trampled through my garden
and you took all of your air out of my lungs

you left, anyway

and you left the door open

you are comparable
to the bluest skies
the smoothest waves
the tallest trees
i will never be able to get rid of you
i feel you everywhere

you must be a part of the earth

i don't remember if it was that night
under the stars in the park
or if it was the night under the moon
in the back of your midsize sedan
but somewhere in between there
i found out the difference between love and lust
your hands reached out for mine
because you weren't used to something so soft
and mine reached out for yours
because you gave me something to hold onto
and i think i got those two confused when
i told you i loved you
somehow i think you took love
and turned it into me being alright
with being sat on a shelf
and played with
when you weren't too busy playing with others
it is my fault for confusing the two
it is my fault for reaching for a body
that i thought was home
and turned out to be nothing more than
a harbor i visited on weekends
it's my fault for believing that same harbor possessed
an ocean with waves that i memorized
so i wouldn't drown again
maybe i remember now
that for you
love existed in the space after lust
and for me
love was the only space we ever existed in
and you never remembered to visit

how long is it going to take you?
i ask

to do what?
he says

forget me
i say

it's okay
you already have somebody
to remember

the saddest conversation i never had

i wonder
when you will get tired
of setting fire to things
you cannot put out

or does it please you?
does it please you
to see other things burn
because you cannot stop the fire
within yourself

teach me
i want to know
how you let go
so easily

my heart controls the sea
and maybe that's why
all of these feelings
felt like oceans
i could never learn to swim in

my heart is my anchor

today the wind asked
when are you going to let it go
i said helplessly
i don't know how to be like you

the rise

beautiful girl
you are blooming
be thankful for the dirt
the world once threw at you
oh
look at how beautiful your colors are
be thankful how the sun shined on you
oh
look at how strong your roots are
be thankful the days it poured on you
beautiful Woman
you are *blooming*

i am growing
more and more into myself
wrapping myself in self love
i am in love
with the thought
that i could possibly be
something more than i once was

i have no urge to possess you
i do not want you to be *mine*
you are not a thing i own
you are not a belonging
i want the privilege to share you
with yourself
and walk side by side
for a lifetime

i step out onto the front porch
from here
i can see your garden
it's desperate, dehydrated, and in need of water
i run inside, fill up the can, run over to you
and water your garden
and every time i step out onto my front porch
i only look for your garden, to see how it is doing
and it needs me
oh, how good it feels to be needed
your garden is blossoming
thriving
flourishing
i take a step back in amazement
and i gaze at the wonder of
what i have done
what i have accomplished
but as i turn around
and set eyes on my own garden
the flowers have wilted
the soil has long drawn up
weeds have taken the place
of where grass used to live
there is no life here
and i hang my head and laugh
how silly of me
to forget to water my own garden
in the midst of watering yours

i crawl in bed
it's warm to the touch
we make love in this bed often
we set it on fire

isn't it funny?
when we were younger
how they would tell us to
run
from this sort of thing

but i am not afraid

i am basking in the heat
i am drenched in love
i am melting from the blaze
into you

i am not afraid

my love
has always been
too heavy
too big
too much
for you
well
i am sorry your hands
were not strong enough
were not big enough
to hold
my love

you were born into a world
where if you are first
and never last
then you are worthy
and enough
where if you get enough attention
or praise
then you are worthy
and enough
where if a man finds you beautiful
then you are worthy
and enough

but Woman
you have always been worthy
you have always been enough
and you always will be

enough

the problem is
you are looking to belong
to someone else
when you don't even
belong to yourself

i built cities
around the men
that tried
to crumble me

she is beautiful
i give you that
intelligent
i give you that
but baby
she is not me
does she make your lips quiver, hard, like i did
does she cradle your heart, soft, like i did
does she make it skip a beat, hard, like i did
does she touch your mind, soft, like i did
does she awaken your soul, hard, like i did
does she hold your head up to the sky, soft,
so you can remember that there is still
light in this world
like i did

she is wonderful
i give you that
but she is no

me

i promise you
one day you will pick yourself up off the floor
you will forget what it sounded like
to hear their footsteps leave you
how they echoed in your heart
swiftly but not gently
and you will start to listen
to your own footsteps
and the places they can take you
and you will fall in love
with yourself
and forget about
waiting for
anyone else's

they may leave you
and when they do
      inhale
      exhale
see
you were breathing
long before them
and you will breathe
long after

they say
do not take chances
stick with what you know
i tell them
my whole world was built on a risk
so why should i not take the chance
to throw myself in
and unearth something magical
all the wonders i have ever held
were based on chances

i am not so much broken
as i am bruised
but wounds heal
and hearts find other pieces
to close up their holes
and i will always stand tall
and *prevail in the morning*

i wake up and i laugh

i was so broken
the night before
i feel
heartache
dried up on my cheeks

but now
i rise

i learn the bird's song
i learn the sunrise's dance
i learn the tide's language
and

i rise

there was a time
i held my head heavy
faith came to me
wrapped me in its arms
and told me not to worry
there was a time
i held my head heavy
hope came to me
and said it would all be okay
there was a time
i held my head heavy
love came to me
and said
try again

i am growing

and i like the way my branches stretch
and how they reach for the sun
but how they also crave the rain

because sometimes it pours
my, does it pour
but the water grows me
too

i am thankful
for the sunlight
and the rain

all the same

i let a man make love to me once
and after
as i lay bare-skinned
and vulnerable
he whispered
you look beautiful
i knew then
what *lust* was

i let a man make love to me once
and after
as i lay with an old t-shirt
frizzed hair
mascara-ran eyes
he whispered
you look beautiful
i knew then
what *love* was

the sand draws me near
and tells me that it is alright
to try
the waves tickle my feet
and tell me that it is alright
to love
the tide pulls me in and under
and tells me that it is alright
to feel
the reef tears me apart
and tells me that it is alright
to break
the ocean spits me back out
onto the shore
and tells me that it is alright
to live

the break-up

i have been told not to love so hard
not to care so much
not to put too much of myself out there
only to be taken advantage of
but i cannot control what others do
maybe they needed my love
maybe they needed my care
maybe they needed me
so i choose to love
anyway
i will always choose to love
anyway

the moon tapped me on the shoulder
and told me to
wait
for the sun will rise again
but for now
to look up
and witness how bright it can still be
in the darkness

i am a river
i have watched living things pass by me
with no intention to pay attention to the beauty
that i possess
i am a river
i have watched living things take from me
with no intention to pay attention to give things back
that i need
i am a river
i have watched living things survive with my aid
with no intention to pay attention to thank me
for saving them

but it is okay
do you hear me?
i said
it is okay

for all the rivers i have ever known
lead straight to the ocean
and if i
can be a small part of something
that grand
then i will be
a river

when i tell you
you will be *okay*
the front line will retreat
the dust will settle
the debris will clear
the wounds will heal
you will still be standing

you will. you will.

a flicker in the night sky
a candle lighting the room
aren't they both just signs
that light
can always be seen
amongst the darkness

this is me
letting you go
and every possible hope
i ever had of *us*
this is me
giving you back to the world
and hoping you find love in someone
like i found it in you

i have arms that do not let go
a heart that forgives too easily
a mind that never stops thinking
legs that run without eyes that look
hands that never stop reaching
but i can be loved
and i will love you
so good, so good

i will not pour concrete on your feet
if you want to fly
i will not confine you to chains
if you want to be free

go,
be free

remember me, while you're at it

i am not looking for someone to complete me
i am a work of art
i am complete and whole
but you can join me
you are a work of art too
imagine how beautiful we would look
hanging upon the walls of life
together

you have
torn her sails
cut her mast
drowned her compass
rummaged her boat
for all you could find
and you are surprised
that she couldn't get to you?
that she couldn't save you
from the storm?

i held your words
to the gas stove top
that is what you get for saying things you do not mean
sometimes your words come out like fire
and pour like lighter fluid
maybe this time
when you get burned
you will finally understand

to all of the
men that i lost
thank you for
uncaging me
i am finally free

well eventually
caterpillars fly too
don't they?

you are not who you are yet

feelings are not supposed to be stuffed down into us
they are not dirty laundry
air them out
let them breathe

you tried to put me in chains
but my wings
are stronger than you think

i will fight for you
but not over you
i will not spill blood
or start a civil war
for you to love me

you were only fascinated
with the idea of me
because when it came time
to tend to my garden
you could not stand
the thorns

you looked upon me
as if i owed you something
as if i owed you one last time
to bestow my love upon you
to broadcast it to the moon
and the stars
i won't
you can go
love owes love nothing
and i am too tongue tied to tell you
too wrapped around the words
that fell out of your mouth
and onto my lap
to try to get you to stay
again

i whisper to the wind
a message to carry to the mountains

i am done trying to move you
and i am not afraid
to climb you anymore

Woman
i know my eyes are not bearing witness
to you tearing yourself apart in that mirror
don't you know you are beautiful?
who told you that you were not?
Woman
please remove all the chains and tangles
that this world has tried to throw on you
they have tried to bring you down
somewhere beneath them
who told you that you should stay there?
Woman
you are made of light
and you start fires that cannot be put out
you are made of all things wonderful
and all things beautiful
who told you to forget that?

loving yourself again
is putting one foot in front
of the other
it is *trying*
even when you believe
you cannot find a reason to

i set it down
i had no use for it anymore

anger

i picked it up
and took it with me
everywhere

forgiveness

the rain
and sun
both
make you
new
again

MAIA

i am beginning to love life
the highs and the lows
the peaks and the troughs

mountains and canyons
are beautiful
aren't they?

the fall, the rise

you said
you regret that you lost me
but darling
i never *belonged* to you
in the first place

you cannot lose what is yours to keep

i will always follow
my compass heart
over my cautious mind

it knows best

i do not want a comfortable love
i want it to be rigid
unable to fit in a box

i want a seed
that we can harvest
roots dug deep into each other
that change the way our branches grow
so when it is all said and done
we can stand back and say
look what we have done

you will not guilt trip me
into falling in your lap once again
and believing the words
that fall out of your mouth
the same ones that made me
trip in the first place

the sun
teaches me
that it is okay to fall
but to always
rise again

you will never be
too much woman
for the right man
and honey
you will never be
too much woman
at all

i have picked myself up a thousand times
i will not make a home out of a place
i did not choose to fall into
i will choose my own home
on my own two feet
and if i should get knocked down again
i will pick myself up a thousand times more
until i choose my own home
with my own two feet

you have to do more
than just exist
existing is
easy
existing is
comfortable
be alive
feel alive
be scared
be fearful
be adventurous
take risks
enjoy the fall
stand up
dust yourself off
and be alive
again
again
again

i told my friends about you
they warned me not to play with fire
i told them
this is not the fire you get burned with
this is the type of fire that sparks
a flame in you that
will not die
this is the type of fire that you can sweep
against your skin without the fear
of third degree burns
only a taste of love
i told them

and now i am here
burning from your love
and i must say
i am enjoying the flames dancing
around my heart and
melting into my skin
i am enjoying the warmth
of the blaze
i have never felt a love
like this

tonight
i am all forgiveness
i am saying sorry
to myself
i am making love
to me

she spent years
searching for a home
in other people
until she finally made
a home
of herself

paint your love all over me
but *please*
don't cover up my brush strokes
i worked hard
to love these

do not pluck me from the ground
i know
i am *soft*
i know
i am *beautiful*
no, do not give me away
leave me here
i am not done
growing yet

the rose

MAIA

the door slams
i look up
you're here
love grins
are you ready to try again?

i choke on my words on their way out
i think so

i have no need to capture a white flag
but i would like you to surrender to my love
and this is not a game by any means
but i am playing for keeps

surrender

these wounds will heal with time
you see
everything does

all the women
that try to dig up your heart
will find me
underneath

permanence

i will not fall to my knees
and bow to you and no
i will not ask of that from you either
i do ask
that we bow our heads together
in church on sundays
and that we still have faith
to try even when we do not feel up to it
that we walk alongside each other
and when we don't see eye to eye
we still manage to stretch our palms
and to love,

anyway

you always wake up and say
tomorrow

what about today?

choose to bathe in me
or choose not to
but my light still shines
with or without you

i am walking through a garden
that i watered all myself
i have proven that these hands
are more capable
than yours used to be

i am falling for myself

MAIA

i have been broken many times

but i am a vessel of light
the more you break me
the more that pours out

i refuse to
be a prisoner
to a love that
left

MAIA

i have realized
i am too much at war with myself
all these cuts and bruises
have come from my own hands
by letting others do with me as they please

to myself, *i am sorry*
i promise i will love you better

i will not hold out
on love just because
it has held out on
me

reciprocity

i will choose the sun's colors over yours
for you never promised to stay
and the sun has always promised
to come back

when you are done
playing in rivers
i'll be the ocean
here waiting for you

plucking the stars
out of someone else's sky
will not make yours
shine any brighter

hatred dims

the fall, the rise

i wonder when you will stop
bathing in fear
and start drenching yourself
in hope

we didn't meet by chance
our stars were aligned
long before we ever looked up

when will this get better?
i asked the rain
and the trees, flowers, and rivers
answered in unison
for they knew what the rain
was capable of
soon

you were not a loss
just a lesson
that i will pack in my bag
and take with me
you will not be considered a loss
you can never lose something
that was not meant for your hands
to hold

i have been all too lost
on what to do with these feelings
i have tried stuffing them down into me
and when that did not suffice
i stuffed them down into hampers
in the laundry room closet

but right now
i make my way to that closet
right now
i let them takeover me
right now
i let them win

you pulled me into the eye of your storm
believing you would leave me broken
but you did not know
i am a hurricane myself

i want to root myself
deep in this world
and bloom
with lessons
from other souls
across it

you will not find me
underneath the wreckage
i will be long gone
by the time you get here
i saved myself
i climbed through the mangled pieces
i stretched my limbs
and i soared
through the clouds
and high above them
i will not be waiting for you
i will not be on my hands and knees
begging nor pleading
for you to save me
you see
i saved myself
i am not a wreck
i am the chapter that comes after it

remember when i asked you
what if i told you i was a flood?
well
i am not the flood
i am what comes after
i am renewal
i am hope
i am strength
i am resilience
i just
am

after the flood

i am
dying
to show you how to
live
you've only been
existing
so far

i'm not going to beg you to stay
the sun does not beg the world
to see its light

if you should decide
to sail away into the sea
in search of calmer waves
do not come back
when your search
runs out

i am breaking free
from who i used to be
i am shedding layers
i am growing new skin
i am bursting through this cocoon
and prevailing

look, i have wings
try and stop me now

you tell me
don't let people in

i laugh
how am i ever supposed to learn?

you're afraid
because you have never
met oceans
as deep as mine
you're afraid
because you might not
know how to swim
in these currents
but i promise this is my love
and this is the only way
i know how to love
this is the only way
i have ever loved

so if you are afraid
stay on the shore
i have no more time
for *shallow lovers*

love me
i wanted to scream
but the words burned up in my throat
and the ashes settled on my heart
before they could reach my lips
and now i remember
that you will only
burn yourself
trying to spark a fire
within someone else

i have shed many skins
to arrive at the one i'm in
i have unraveled
and consumed myself
again and again
in new skin
i have grown accustomed to it
but it is only temporary
it stays in the guest room
until the other arrives
to take its place
they all do
but i am content
for i know
there will be many skins
after this one
but for now
i will dance in this skin
i will thrive in this skin
i will love in this skin
i will live
in this skin

you began to climb over my walls
wide eyed and full of heart
but soon, you grew tired
you perched yourself at the top
looking down upon me
as if you weren't sure enough
to press on
i wondered what you were thinking
i wondered if you would turn back
but i will never convince a man
that it is worth it
to climb over the walls
that the world helped me build
i will never convince a man
that it is worth it
to love me

do not feel sorry for me
i am a Woman
i laugh at scars
converse with the moon
throw my hands up in love
drag my body through wars
and heal again but
i am a Woman
and a Warrior
and i rise

the backbone

i am all but understood
when i preach to them
about unconditional love

*wh*y, they say
why not, i ask

broken barriers

i savored the honey
that the bees were kind enough
to leave behind for me

life is soft in that way
receiving the sweetness of life
from things
that are supposed to sting

now i know why
the honey tasted a lot
like love

you will be searching forever
to find someone
to fill a hole in you
that you are meant to fill
yourself

when you walked away
a piece of me left with you
and the girl i was
when i was with you
left too
i am proud to say
i don't know her anymore
i am proud to say
i am me, now

i understand now
i loved you in ways
that you couldn't love yourself
i understand that the magnitude
of my heart made you feel weak
and poked at your masculinity
i understand that you had to run
and make me question my worth
to save it

breaking - healing

they are one in the same

he asked
do you write poetry for me?
i said
no
i write poetry about you

these words are for me to keep
you just get to feel them

i will still give
in spite of
what they do not
give back

and it gives me comfort to know
that even if we are not standing side by side
we are under the same sky
and that is enough for me

some nights
i embrace the damage
that has been done to me
i trace my finger along
my scars and rejoice in the
fact of knowing that i heal
beautifully

you are afraid to show me your scars
as if they don't mean
even the deepest of wounds
can be healed

i walked outside
and the trees
were shedding their leaves
the crunching under my feet
sounded like goodbyes
and if they can let go
i can too

the dust has settled
i am rising up from the ashes
for once
i don't need you to save me
and i want you to know
you can't break me anymore

you did not know what to do
with your sadness
so you turned it into pain
and poured it into others
i turned mine into love
and poured it into you

i promise you
the nectar of this life
is sweet
don't be afraid
to taste it

there is beauty
in the breaking
there is joy
in renewal

i am now soaring over
the same mountains i tried to move
this is what happens
when you harness the power
that once tried to destroy you

you left
and suddenly
i wasn't so broken anymore
it wasn't the door closing
but one opening
and i am ready to bask
in all of the possibilities
that walk through it

i am taking it back
all the love i poured into you

it's mine now
it belongs to me

to the man
that made me feel part of a whole
i am sorry
you thought i was a piece
of you
as if *you* birthed *me*
i am a whole
and i will never be
just a piece

in that moment
i realized that the beauty
in believing you need someone
is finally understanding
that you don't

i cannot love you
with my heart half empty
you must pour into me
too

love is not giving
someone the world
and getting upset when
they fall in love with it

it is giving someone the world
and loving them even if
they walk away from you
for it

yes
there is brokenness
but there is love here
too

i let you go
and now i have a backbone
my spine grew back
it was tired of carrying
the weight of us

i don't
have your love
but at least
i still have
my own

tell me
i want to know
who ripped you open
and told you
that you were so
undeserving of love?

i just know God himself
planted you in my heart
you were always made
to bloom for me
i was always the soil
to help you rise

so i will continue
to plant seeds of kindness
come take a look
at this garden

see how love thrives here

if you cannot love me
without ropes around your heart
and cement feet
then do not love me
at all

one day
i will have a love
that loves me
someday
love
will love me back

the day is coming

some men
don't know how
to love a woman
that loves herself

i found
the best parts
of me
when you left

i shouted up to the sky
why me
it cried with me in return
but then it stopped
the sun came out
a rainbow formed

heartbreak is not the end
after all

some arms
are not meant to catch you

love, anyway

sometimes i forget
that i am allowed
to break

i must remember

love is not my enemy

thank you for treating me
as if i was ordinary
now i know that
i am extraordinary

nothing was lost
when you left
everything, everything
was gained

i once
defined myself
by the way
i let a man
love me

i will never
be foolish again

how silly of me
to forget that i am
the love of my life

i have written many lines
about feeling empty
but those feelings
were only temporary
for i now know
i am never alone
with you

God

all i can do
raise up my hands
and thank *God*
for He sent hope to me
for He sent faith to me
for He sent grace to me
for He sent all the things
i needed the most
that i now possess
he sent the rain to me
the sun, the moon
and the stars
the oceans and the skies
and He taught me how to listen
to them
for in them
i found *Him*

thank you

sunsets are
undoubtedly
my favorite time of day
it gives me comfort to know that
if something so heavy
can fall
and rise again
beautifully
with poise
and grace
then i
with my heavy heart
can too

the sun's weight

acknowledgments

i want to take this time to acknowledge all of the ones who helped me on this journey to the birth of my first collection of my heart on paper.

thank you to my parents for always encouraging me to write as a child and making it known that i can aspire to be whatever i choose. thank you to my friends who supported me throughout this process. thank you for being patient with me. thank you to pride nyasha mapfumo for creating a beautiful cover and illustrations that fit this book so perfectly. thank you to the readers, who allow me to bear my soul and connect with me on more levels than one. thank you to the souls that i wrote about throughout this book. if it weren't for you, i would never have learned important lessons.

thank you for the love, the hurt, and the healing.

about the author

maia is a writer who fell in love with the art of
poetry. she always wrote short stories as a young
child. words always came easier that way. she dreams
to write and travel the world wishing to share her
soul with others. she believes that we could all learn
from each other. she knows that the one thing that
makes us the same is that, at the core, we all want
love. we all want to love immensely and be loved in
returned. but sometimes, we let go of ourselves in
wanting to receive that love that we so deeply crave.
she is a woman with a longing to change the world
while creating art in the form of words.

the fall, the rise is her debut poetry and prose
collection dealing with heartbreak and losing
yourself in love but rising up to fall in love with
yourself.